HAL LEONARD STUDENT PIANO LIBRARY

EARLY ADVANCED

Piano Recital Showcase
ROMANTIC INSPIRATIONS

8 ORIGINAL PIANO SOLOS

CONTENTS

Copyright © 2010 by HAL LEONARD CORPORATION
International Copyright Secured All Rights Reserved

ISBN 978-1-4234-7575-0

HAL•LEONARD®
CORPORATION
7777 W. BLUEMOUND RD. P.O. BOX 13819 MILWAUKEE, WI 53213

In Australia Contact:
Hal Leonard Australia Pty. Ltd.
4 Lentara Court
Cheltenham, Victoria, 3192 Australia
Email: ausadmin@halleonard.com.au

Visit Hal Leonard Online at
www.halleonard.com

Prelude No. 1

Carol Klose

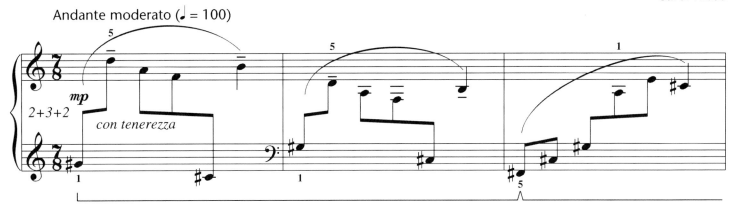

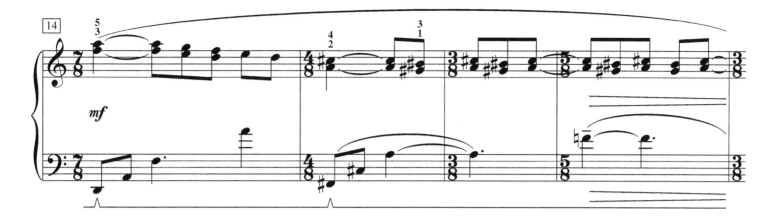

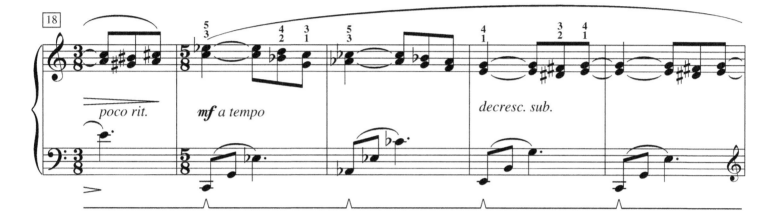

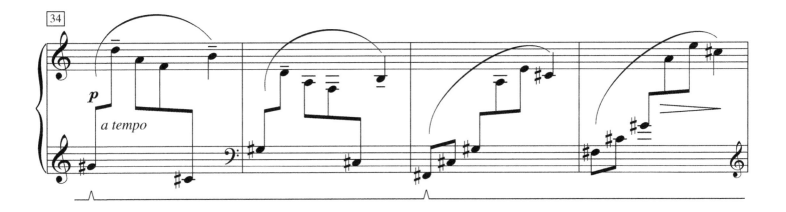

Poco più mosso

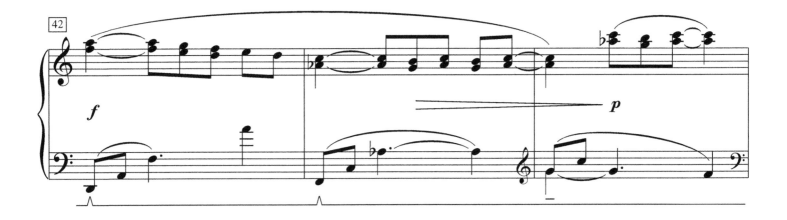

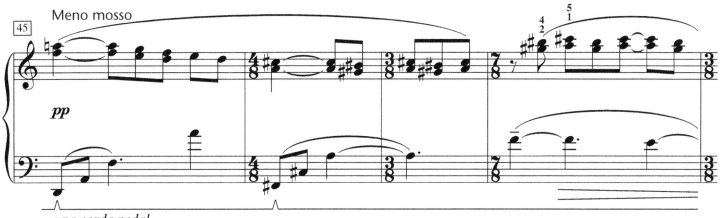

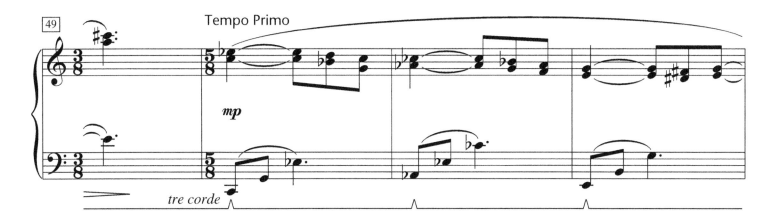

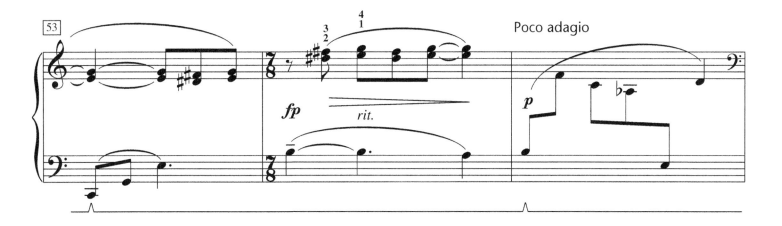

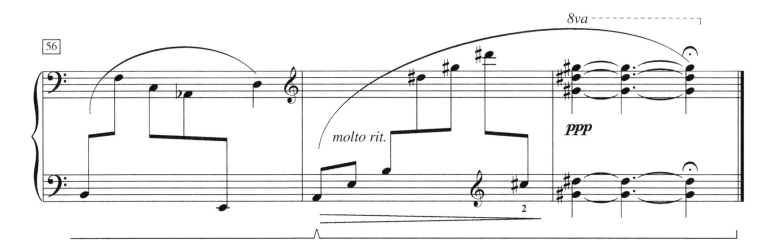

Rapsodie

Eugénie Rocherolle

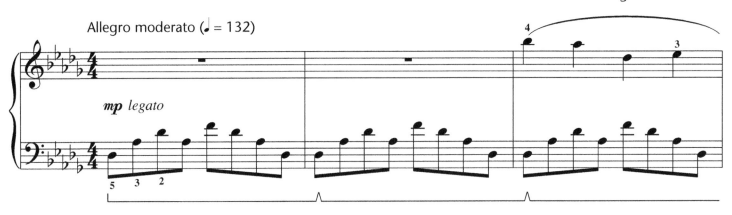

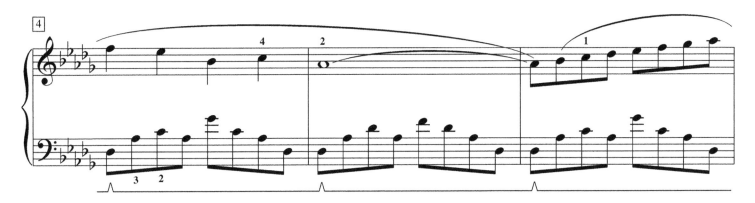

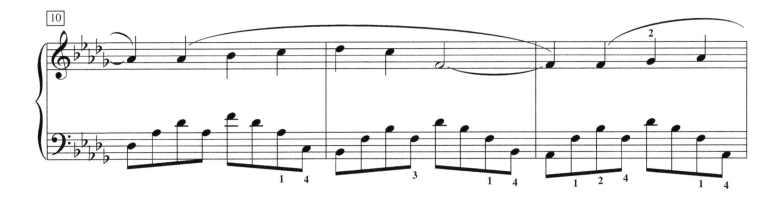

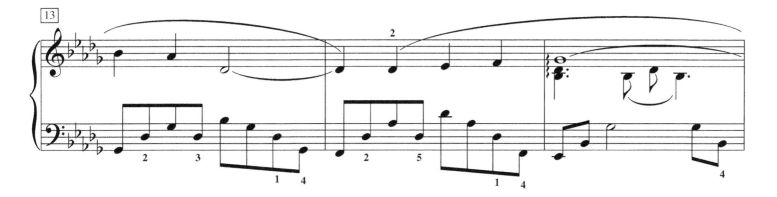

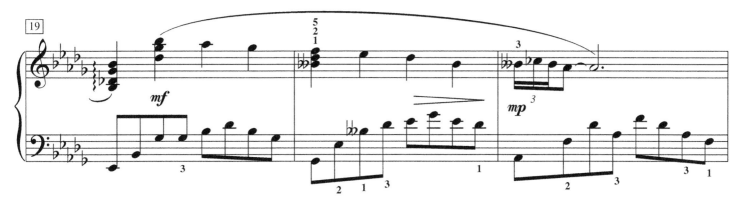

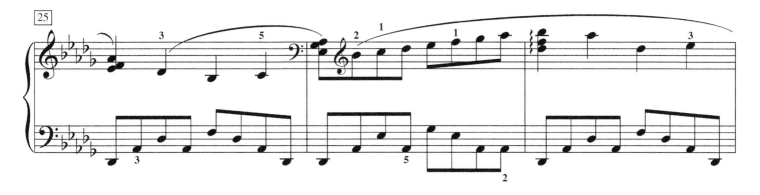

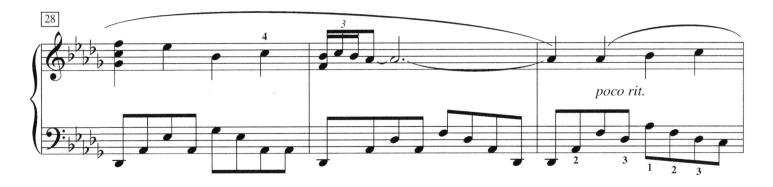

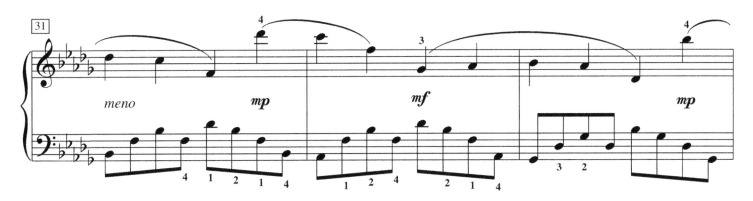

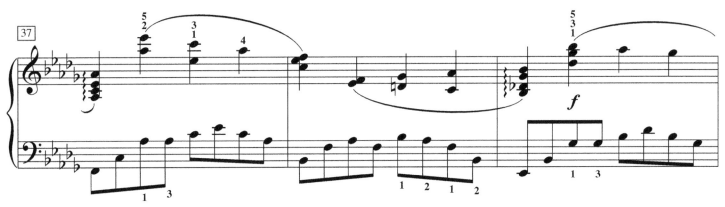

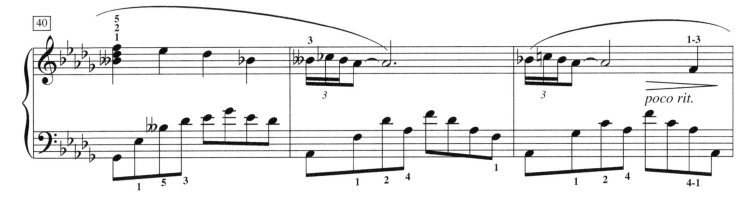

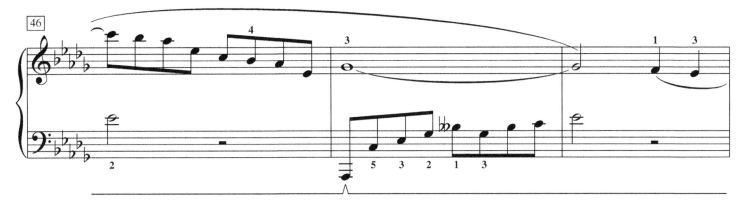

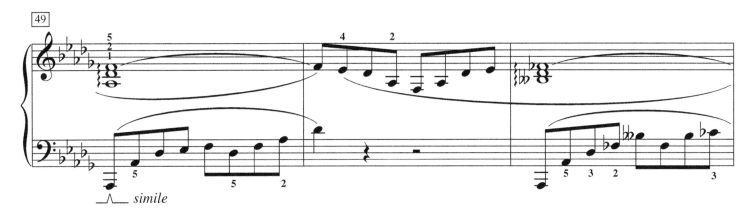

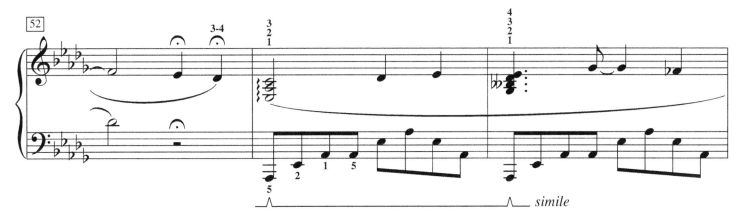

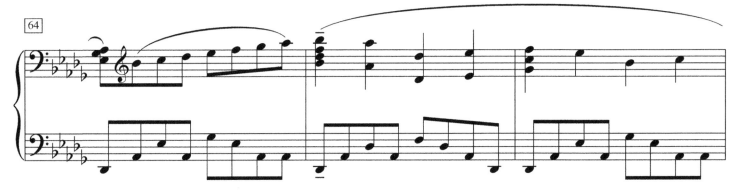

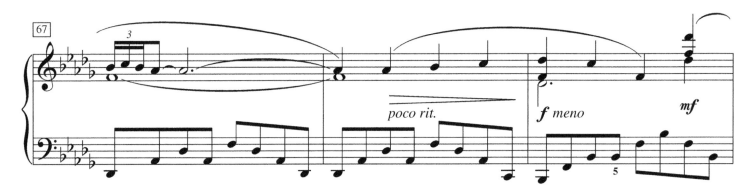

10

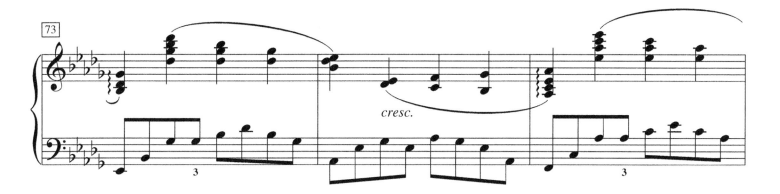

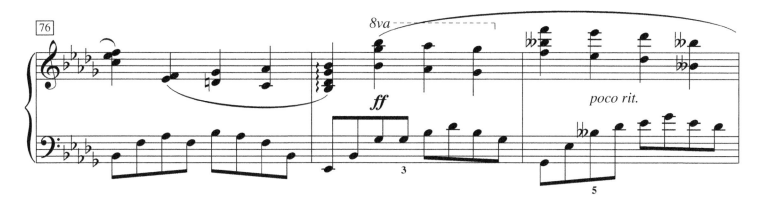

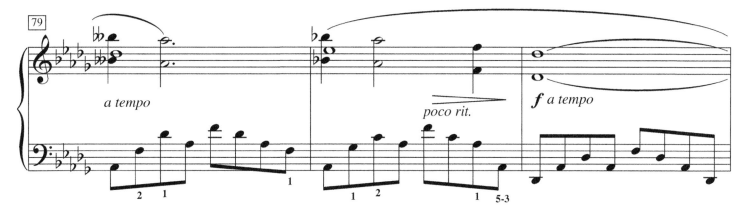

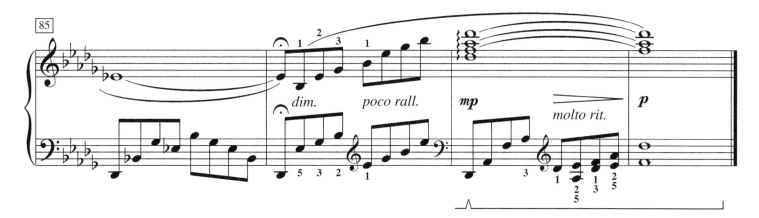

11

Nocturne d'Esprit

Jennifer Linn

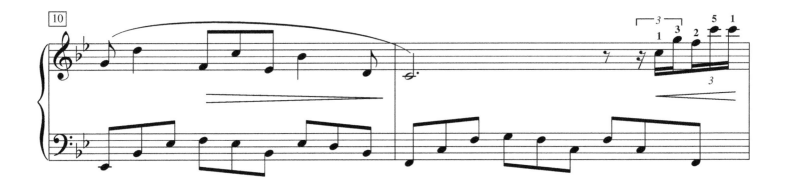

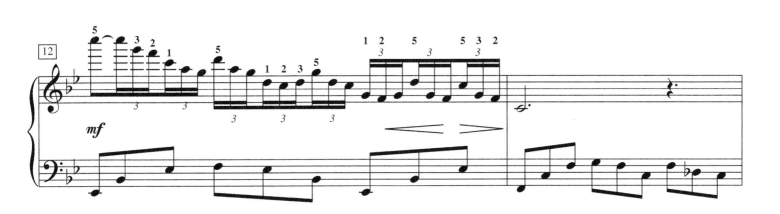

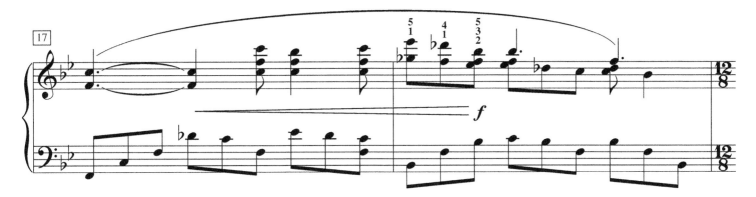

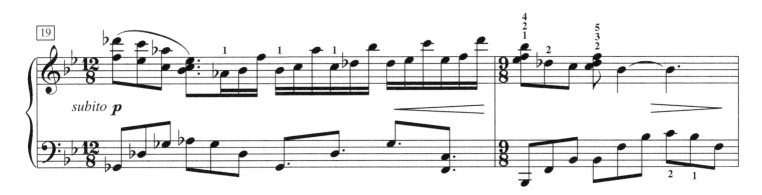

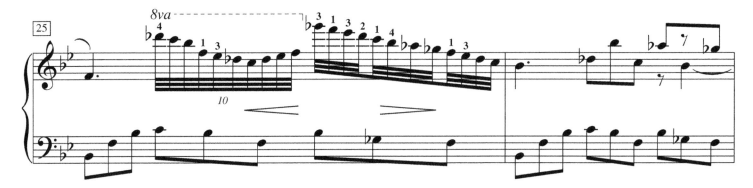

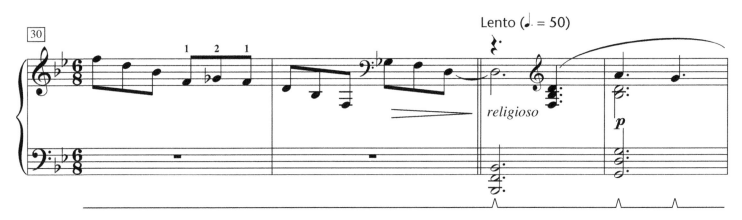

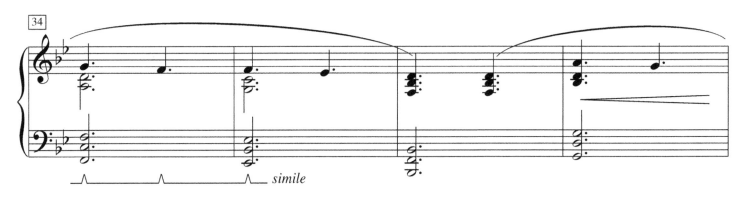

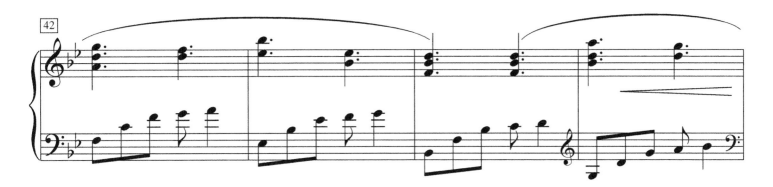

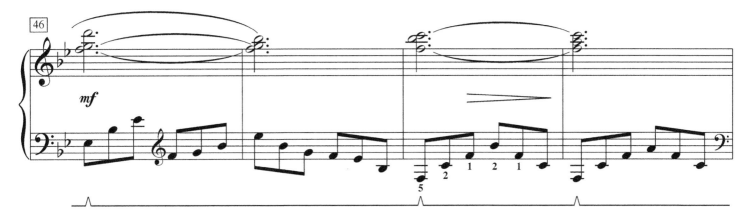

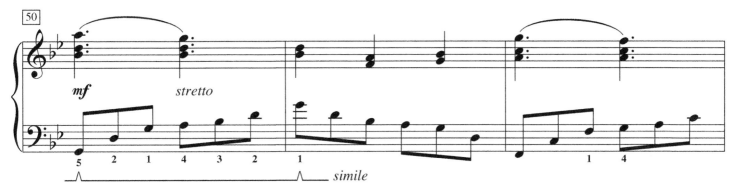

15

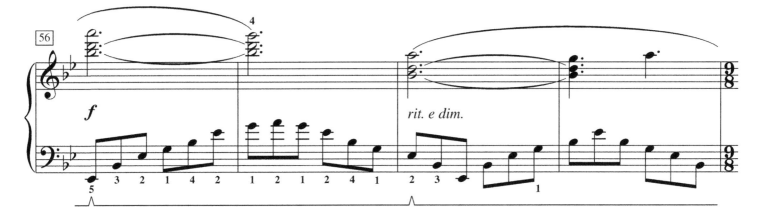

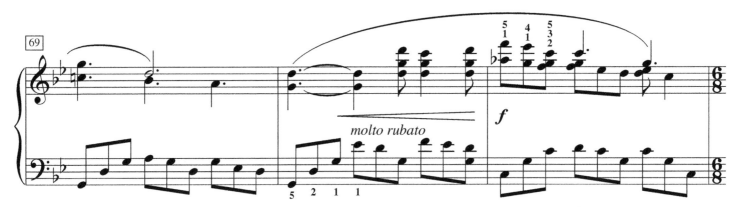

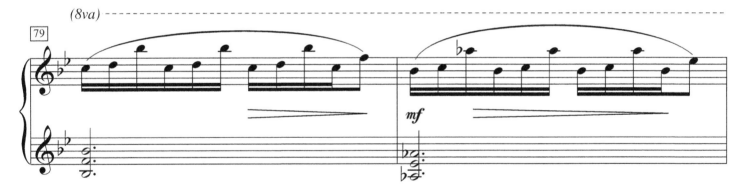

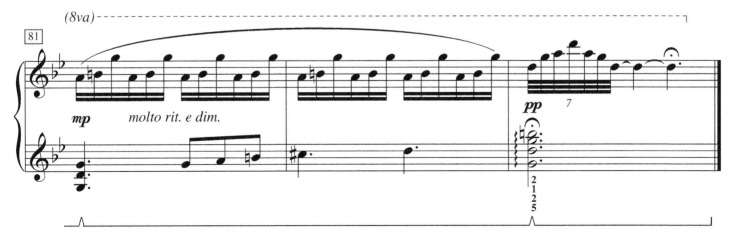

Valse d'Automne

Christos Tsitsaros

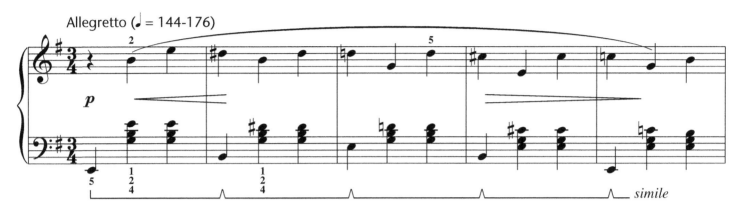

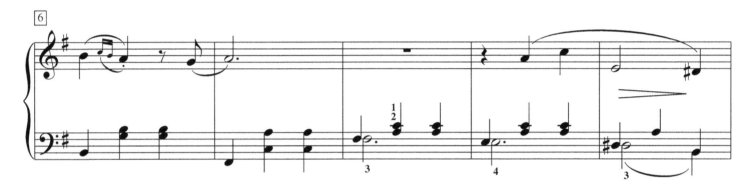

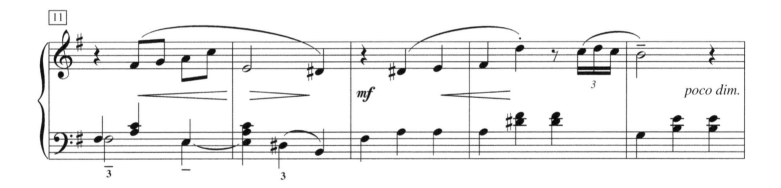

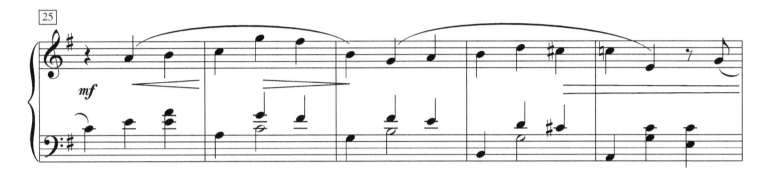

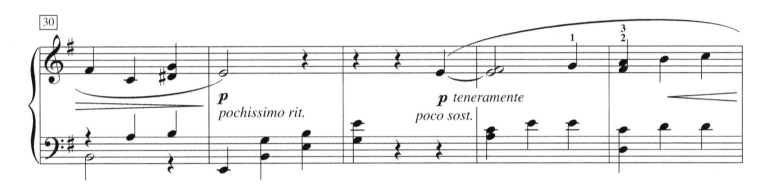

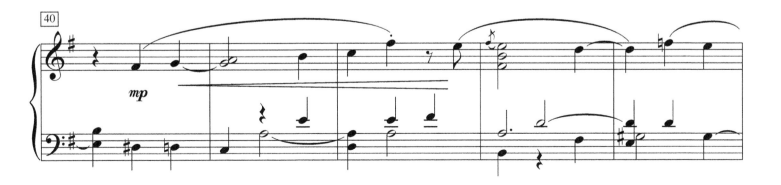

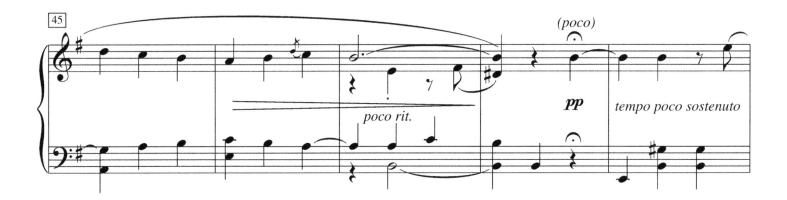

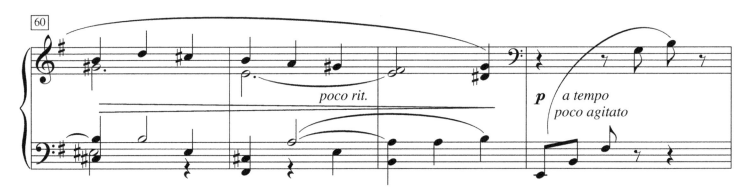

20

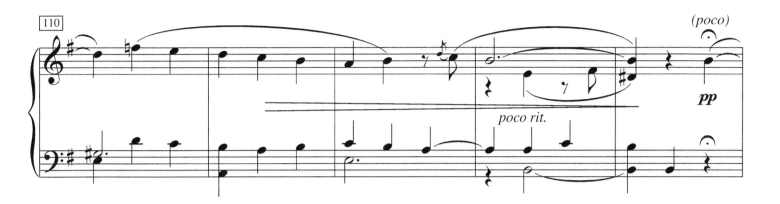

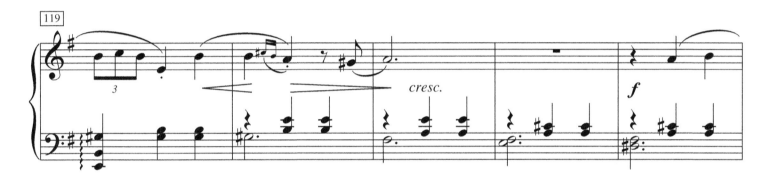

Rondo Capriccioso

Carol Klose

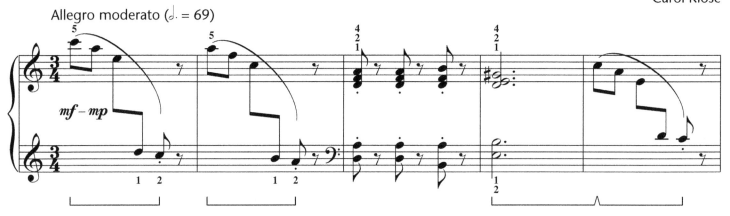

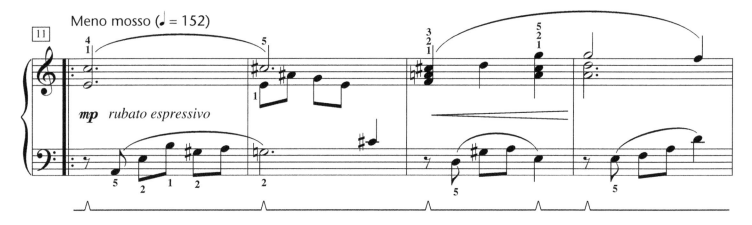

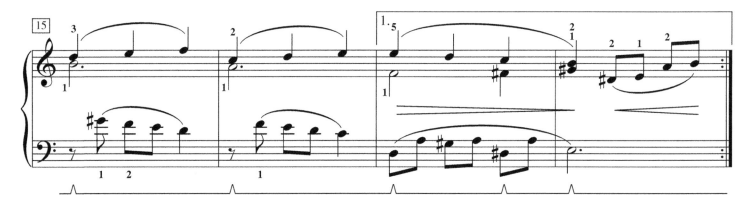

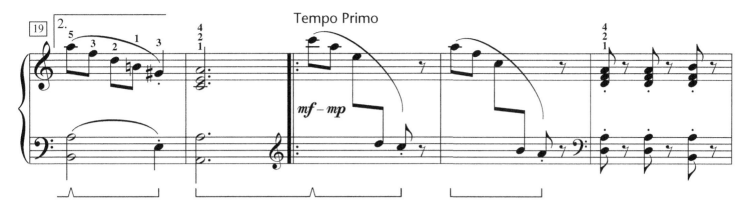

Tempo Primo

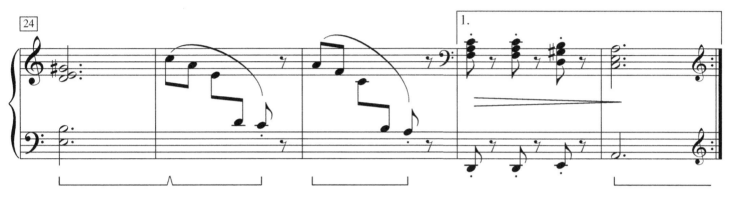

Andante espressivo (♩ = c. 144)

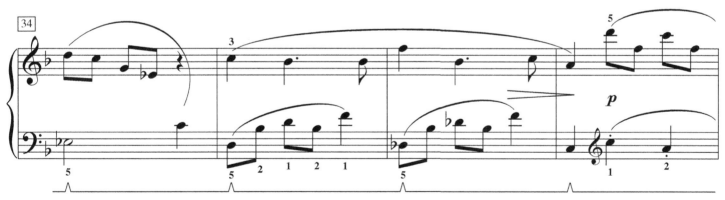

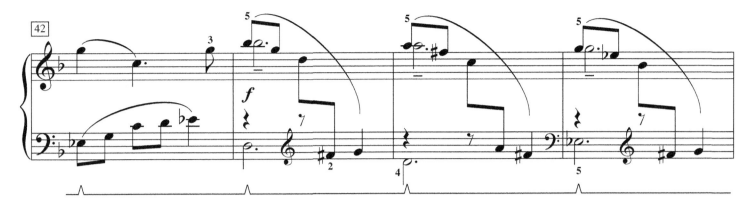

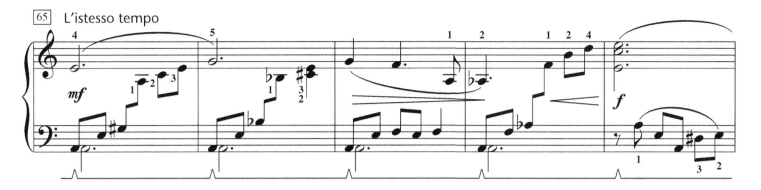

L'istesso tempo

(♩. = 52)

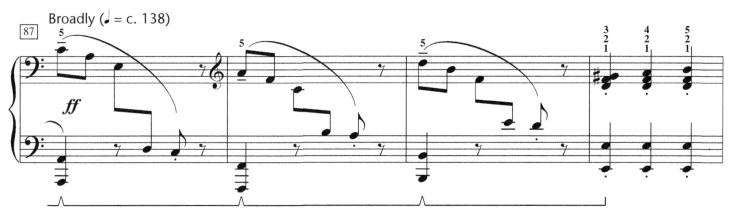

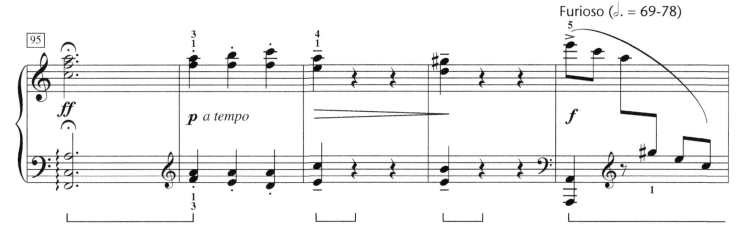

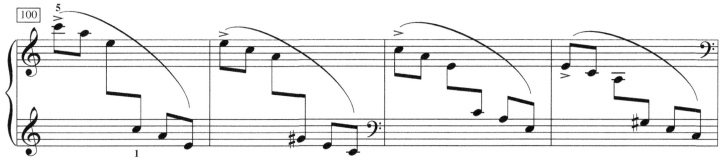

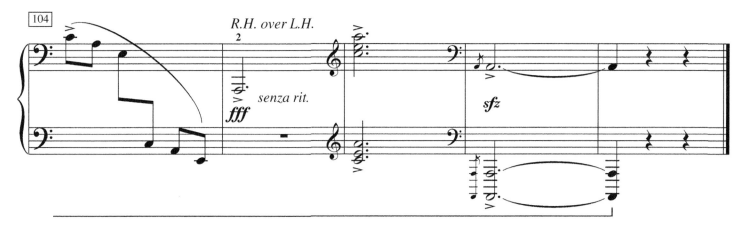

Arabesque

Jennifer Linn

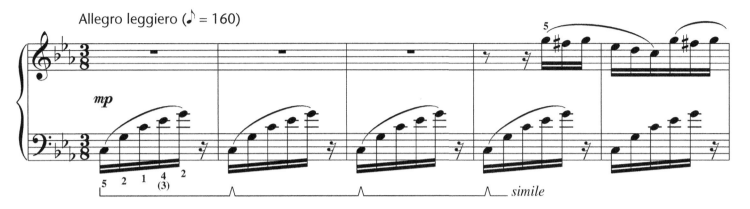

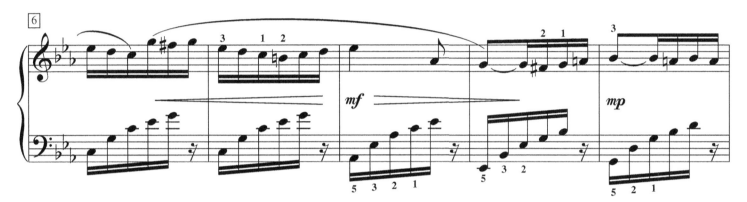

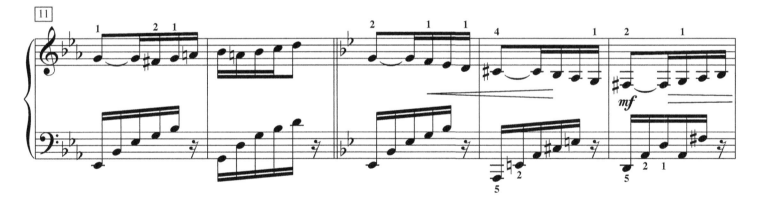

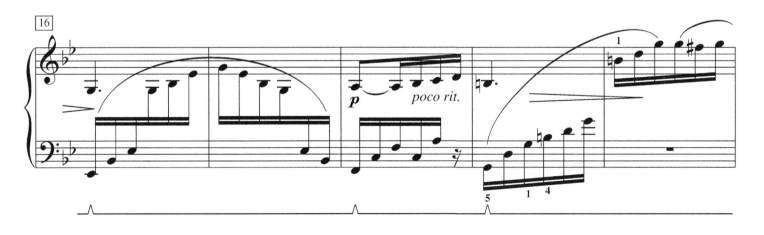

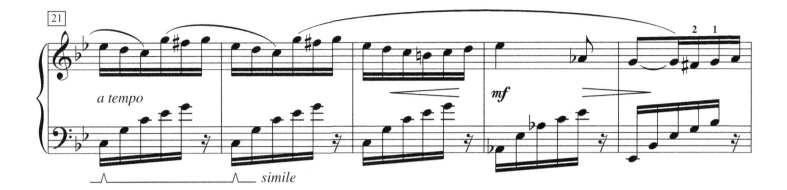

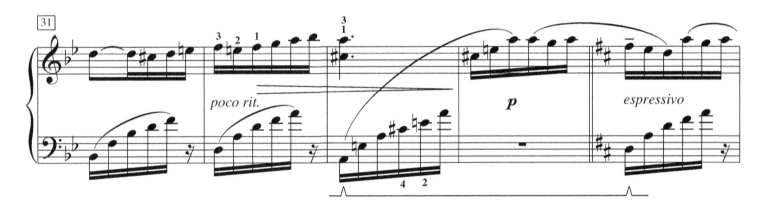

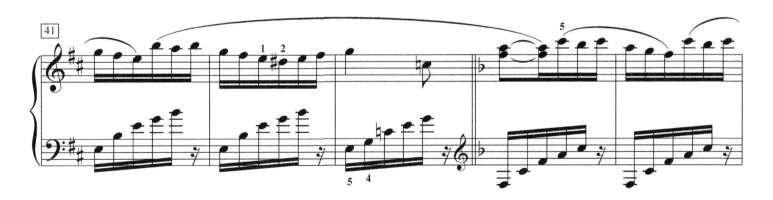

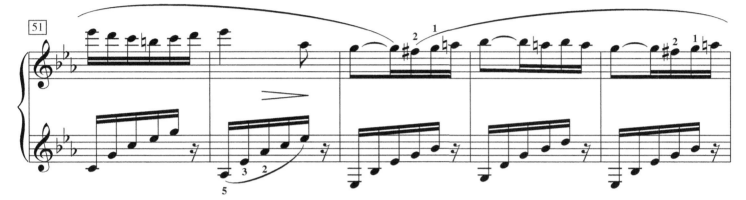

Cantabile (♪ = 120)

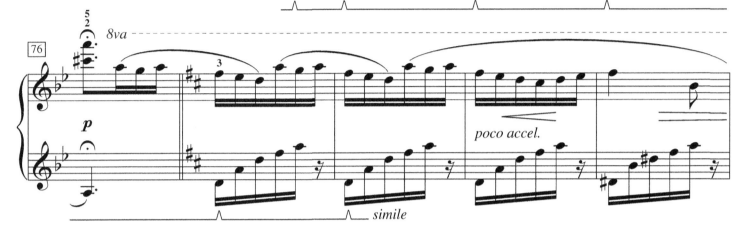

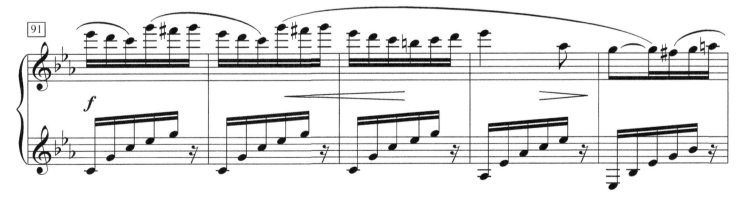

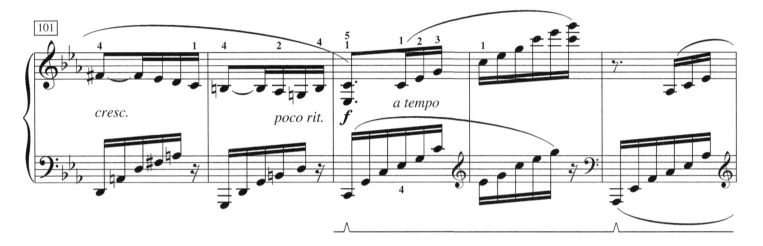

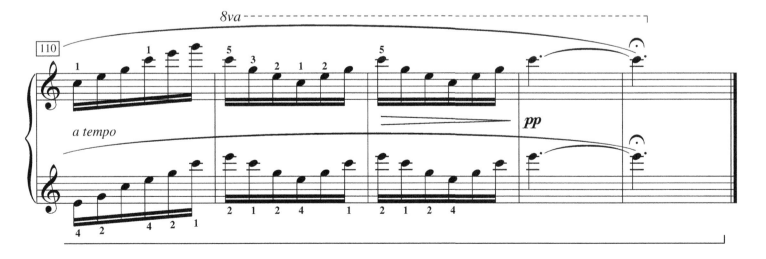

Nocturne

Christos Tsitsaros

Lento ma non troppo (♩ = 80)

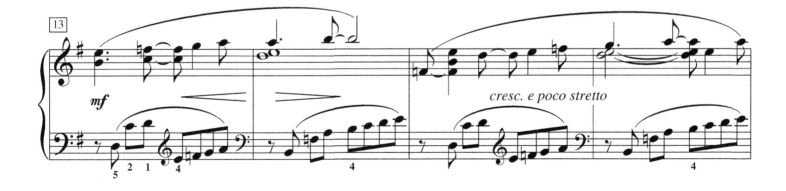

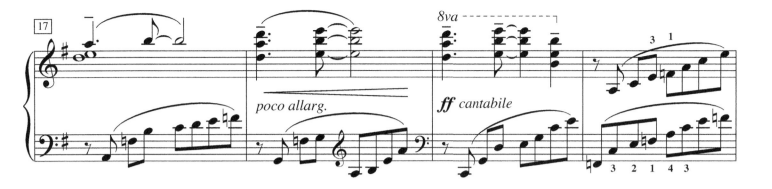

Poco più mosso (♩ = 80)

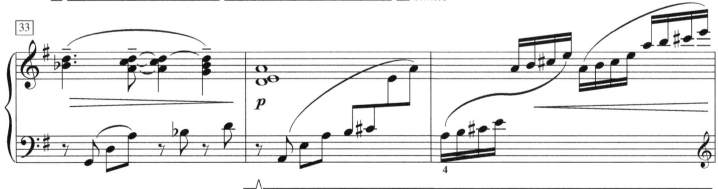

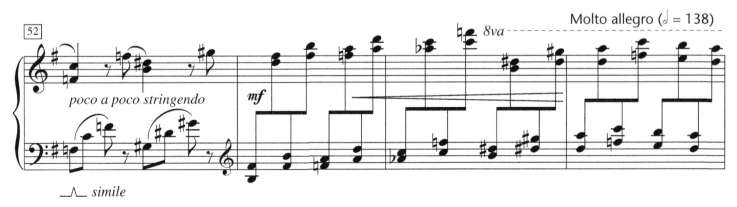

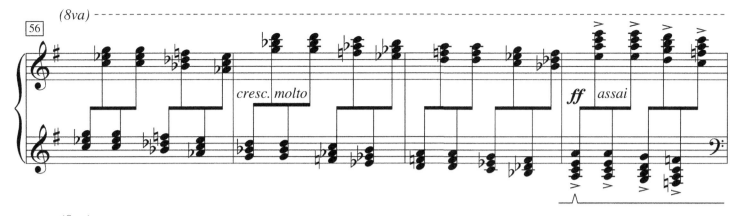

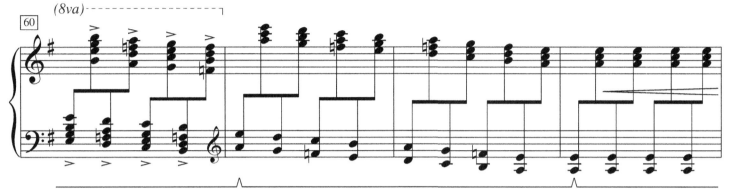

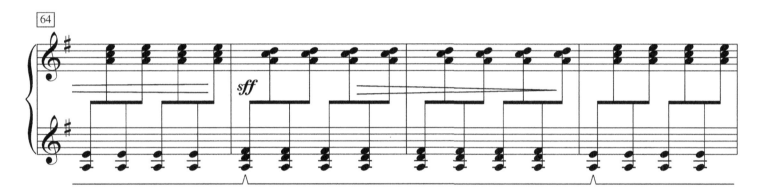

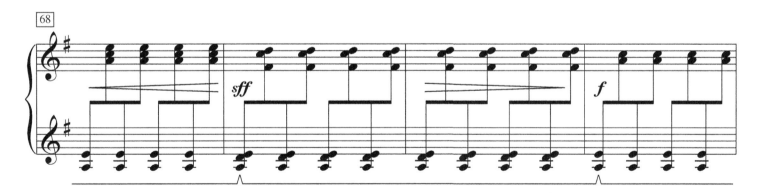

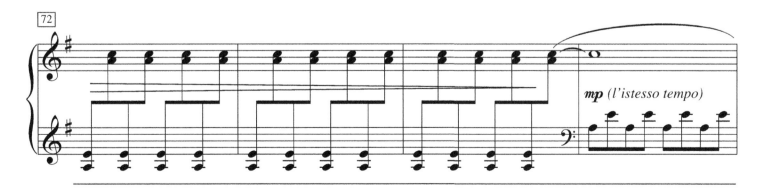

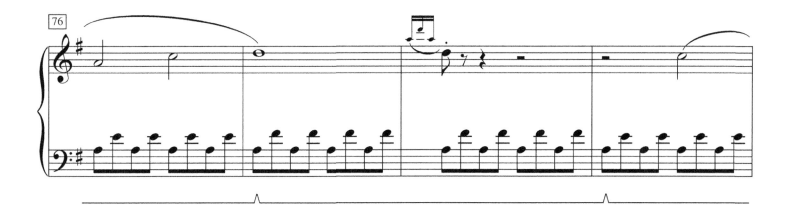

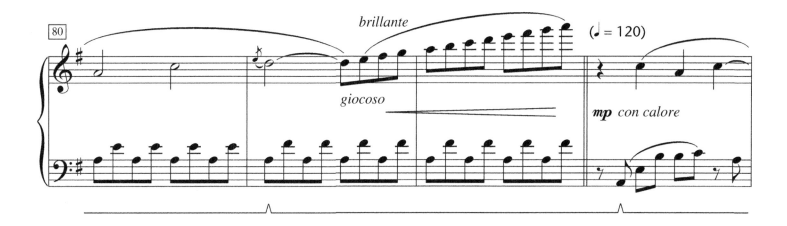

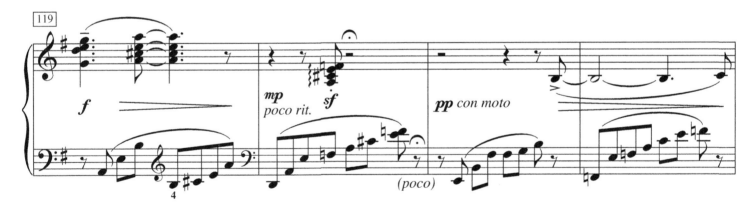

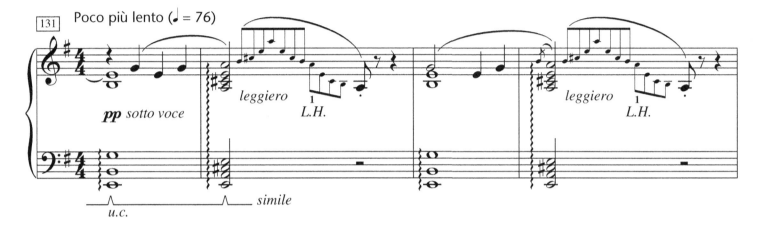

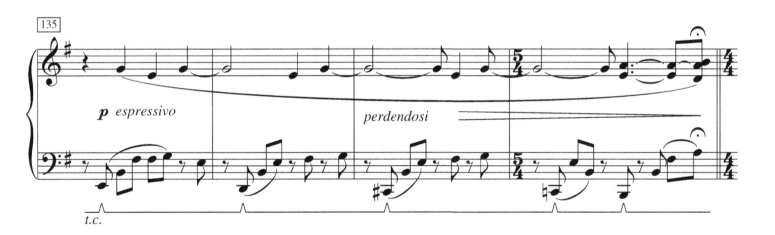

41

Journey's End

In memory of Michael "Longbow" Russell

Eugénie Rocherolle

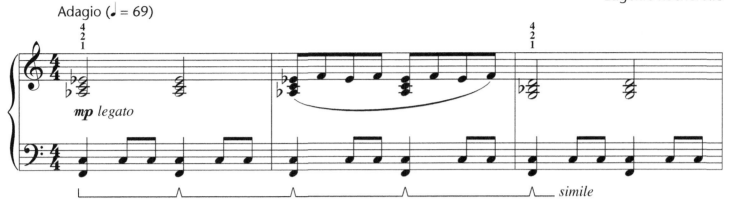

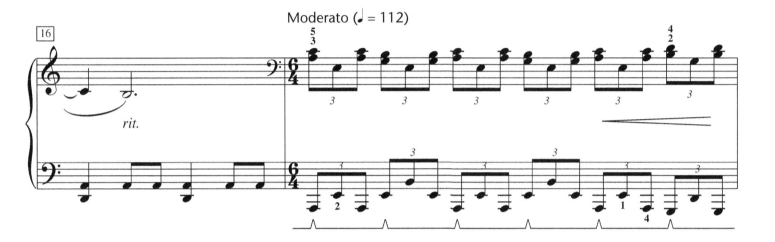

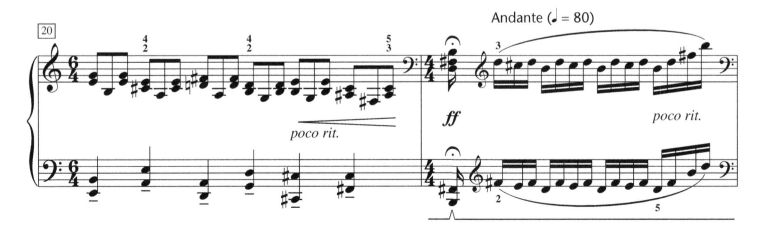

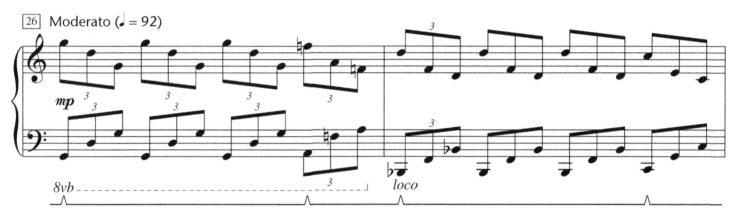

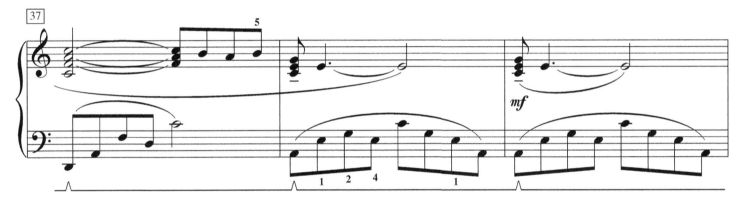

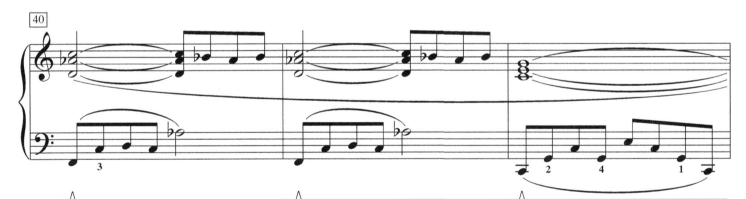

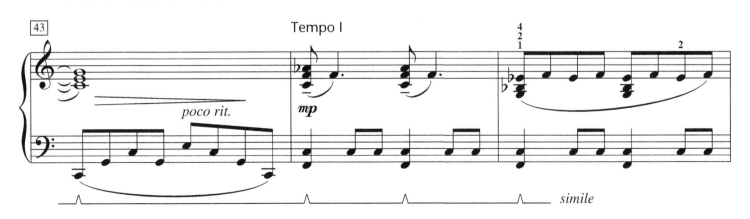

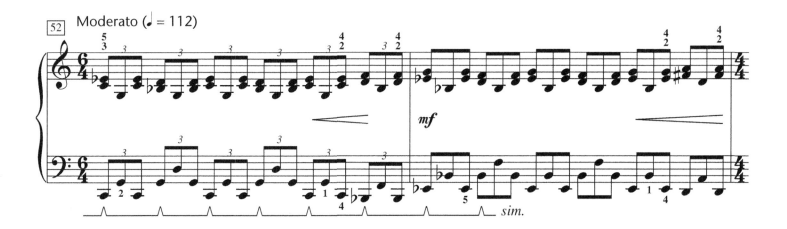

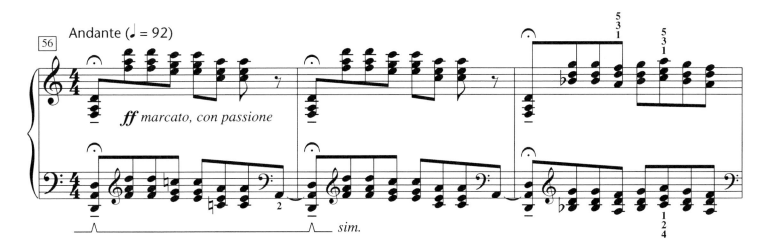

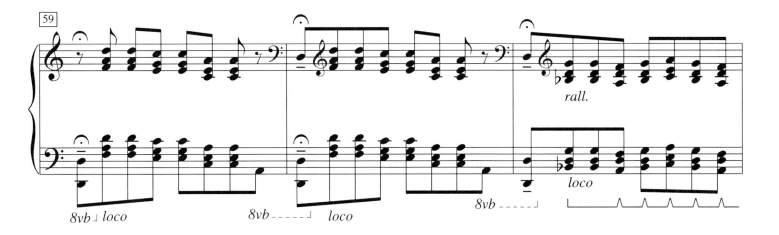

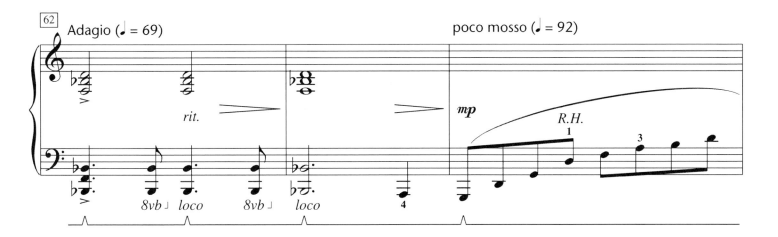

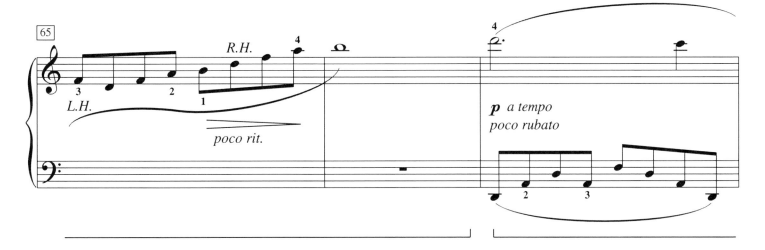

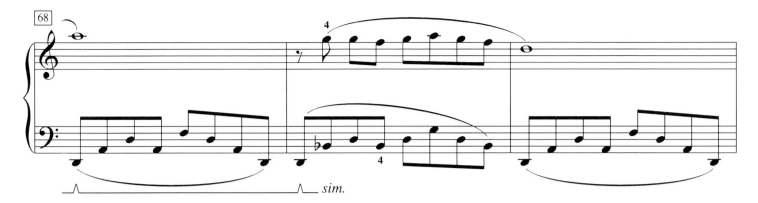

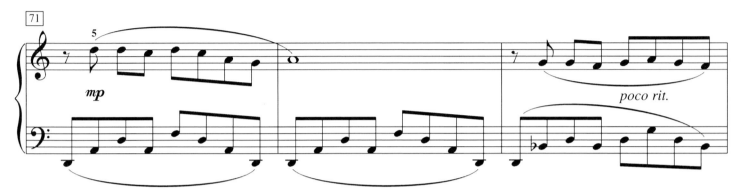

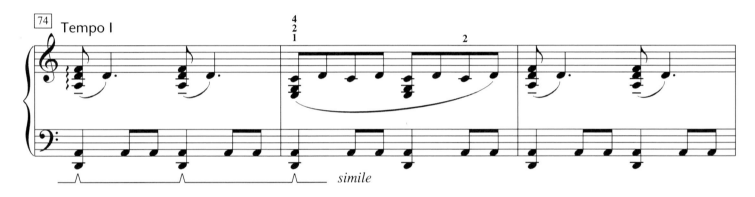

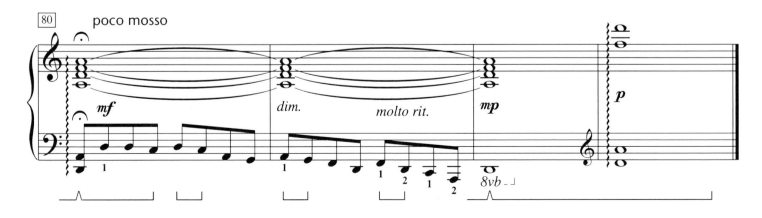